THIS PERFECT LIFE

The Miami University Press Poetry Series
General Editor: James Reiss

THIS PERFECT LIFE

Poems
by

KATE KNAPP JOHNSON

Miami University Press
Oxford, Ohio

Library of Congress Cataloging-in-Publication Data

Johnson, Kate Knapp
    This Perfect Life: poems / by Kate Knapp Johnson.
        p. cm.— (The Miami University Press poetry series)
    ISBN 1-881163-04-0. —ISBN 1-881163-05-9 (paper)
    I. Title. II. Series.
    811'.54—dc20   93-13790
                                                             CIP

Printed by Cushing-Malloy, Inc., Ann Arbor, MI.

The paper in this book meets the guidelines
for permanence and durability of the Committee
on Production Guidelines for Book Longevity
of the Council on Library Resources. ∞

Printed in the U.S.A.

9 8 7 6 5 4 3 2 1

This book is dedicated to Doug, and to Peter.

ACKNOWLEDGMENTS

The author wishes to acknowledge the editors of <u>DECADE</u> (NEW LETTERS), ONE MEADWAY, and D Magazine in which some of these poems have appeared. I would also like to thank the New York Foundation of the Arts for a grant which supported the writing of a number of these poems.

The poem, SUIT OF LIGHT, is dedicated to Cathy Appel and Marion Woodman.

Special thanks to my family, to Thomas Lux, James Davis, and to the faculty and students at Sarah Lawrence College for their help and kindness.

CONTENTS

TWO

ONE

.... To be a fool
takes devotion of the most pigheaded sort.
You have to want one thing in the wrong place
so badly you make it a way of life.

—Tess Gallagher

UNTITLED

It is not white. Cannot
float. It doesn't think there are so many
flowers in this garden.
It is the iron darkness
from inside. Honest, but liable
to snag in the enemy's fat hand.
It's the goat, shivering dog, bad
girl. The unwanted,
Different. It is anything
different.

What is the soul? Shame,
they said. You should be ashamed.

THERAPY

I pity Christ's victims—the ones
he made walk, the blind
who had to see. What
is given up? Every healing is a kiss:
goodbye, dear feathers
of infirmity. Now I am told
to look, to account
for my own past, which changes
the life ahead of me. Willowy sinews
cramp behind the eyes—so bright
and strange to walk
with those who simply walk
in the unadorned world.

CLOTHILDE

So childhood rooms are gone, refashioned
into parlors and dens. The repeating wallpaper
of blue George Washingtons standing in his boats
has been stripped, painted white and windows curtained.
I remember lying on my brother's bed asking how come
boys get generals and I get pink
walls, pink border with a pink picture
of a rabbit, inscribed: Be quick
as a bunny?

I was not quick as a bunny—like Clothilde
I got nailed. Her neck
was bruised, wet when our dog
took her in his mouth. We couldn't get Cloe out
from under the governess's bed. I threw down
pieces of donuts, crumbs
all over the rug. My brothers said
this was stupid: rabbits
don't eat donuts. The thing was
Cloe did. If she'd been there
Mother would've killed us all.

Did she ever want
to kill us? I mean did we
ruin something for her? A child
has to steal her life
from her parents. A child has to
stick a bone out the bars of the cage
instead of her arm so the witch won't
eat her up, has to lie

and say the oven's not lit
so when the witch looks
she can shove her in and slam the door . . . .

You know it can't be enough
but you go on, you keep striking
your head with that spoon—studying,
swimming, correcting
your backhand. Dieting, dieting. . . .
I wanted to be perfect
for her. I wanted to be so fucking wonderful.

But somewhere at the end of childhood
I needed a rest.
I used to hike in the pine
forest behind the barns.
Like I could get far enough away
when I wanted to race home, pink,
quick, just once. God
I loved her. At the end of childhood
I needed a long sleep.

I used to think Mother was away
an awful lot. When she came home
she'd bring us things. I got
a plastic snowman. You'd put ice

in his hat and turn the knob
on his stomach until it churned out
snow. . . . It ought to be a child's birthright
to be loved.
It ought to be a law.

I was older when I cut myself. It wasn't so much
to die as to feel. But I felt shame.
My parents were ashamed and forbade me
to tell my brothers.

My brothers live in houses; they have two
children each and furniture
with slipcovers. I live in this farmhouse, old, nice
enough, but the front doorknob keeps coming off in my hand,
the gas line to the water heater is clogged, goes on
and off like an emotion
lodged in the thicket of a brain.
To have this life of mine,
to have any life, I must
kill her, now, like this, shove her in and slam
the oven door. It takes everything
out of me. Smoke
and smell of flesh and hair. This walking away.
It takes everything.

PORCH

In a very general sense
I am always *here*, implant
of this wicker chair, watching homebound
traffic and afraid
to take the hornets' nests
from the eaves in case they
are what's been holding up the porch
all these years. Literally,
philosophically, I feel "here"—sui
generis, the uncaused
cause of why
we're apart, the fruit trees snowy,
fig unsure of its new soil, of its own appeal.
It traveled in a box on a train
eleven days. I was possessed
by this idea, ordering it
in February, waiting three months, imagining it, as love
travels towards or away
from reach without our knowing. More
like Eckhart than Augustine unfortunately, I sit
and from here can see
the fig's shiny leaves, late day light
in them, a face
in a silver pitcher. . . . We are right

to be separate; the porch,
an old witness with her heart
of webs and hooks, knows
being right is far
from being happy. Fig
shines. Evening bird
sings. Splits her beak, in fact,
to sing.

POSSUM

This apparent lack
of organization, the addled
look on my face? What
can you expect from me
when I seem to have lost
all bearing, persimmon juice
between my claws? The possum,
sweet-faced and foetid marsupial, survives
by acting dead. It's surviving
that keeps me paralyzed too,
wheel-chaired to this lifelong role
of the cheerful, but vacuous
species. Obsequious,
instinctive as the rodent
who buries her nose in her butt, I do
what I do to stay alive,
hoping the predators, the big
ones will merely sniff or nudge and trundle off.
I imagine it costs
the possum nothing, playing dead; in fact,
it saves her skin—but all my acting
vague, not quite
capable?—it's a glitch
in the notion of survival, human
error: you pay with your life
to live.

COMMITMENT

In forty six days I'm getting married, and isn't it funny
how, once you've got the world backwards,
it continues to be so? All spine and no breast
is the way you would put it
from your little abode
in Brooklyn. *I know you,* know
you must hate it there, Mister
City Life, Mister. . . . It is not the sadness
that affects me so much
as the messiness of going on
without you. Memories are not

affordable, but some thing
must pull the cart of my life along. Perhaps
you have thrown away
the bright straw birds we made, the wooden donkey
we laughed at, changed with our laughter
into a symbol of lastingness. . . . What
could possibly last? Only the puzzlement
over what went wrong
and my memory of it, my commitment
to that wrongness.

WHAT'S LEFT

Eight, or eighty-eight
hundred, in one fortnight,
in one day, I can eat
eighteen boxes of pecan sandies. Food

is the enchantress—it coos; it bares its nipples
and brays in my ear. It even says
it loves me. Makes me feel good. I tell you
I feel so bad and lost I have to eat some more
to keep the world and you,
my friends, away. . . . Amazing

food: here it is
in the freezer, there it is
in the toilet. A miracle
of transubstantiation, lovely
hatchet-blow, absent bosom
of my absent mother. How

did it slowly
suddenly happen
that all my life began to spin
around this one caloric center, this big
fat F, the fib
that keeps my loneliness at bay?

I close the door
to eat, slam out
the one I love, poor him.
I get so large he can't get close
and then so thin
I'm barely here at all, so sick
he has to call a nurse,

a priest. . . . Of all the sadnesses, this is the one
I thought would make me happy: this
cherry soda, this box of melting
Haagen Dazs and when I'm done
I'll wipe my mouth, climb inside
my own heart's farthest
emptiness, wishing
I could eat that, too.

SUIT OF LIGHT

Lying here, I honestly can't tell you
if it's the radiator making late winter
spittle noises or my own stomach, acid
with emptiness. That's how far
I've come, how many worlds
have arrived between my soul and its living
quarters. The other day
I saw this woman, sort of
round, soft red
hair, heated with talk, swinging
her caftan arms—and there was light

in her, feet
of herself solidly inside
her feet, bowl
of the groin trembling
from being dipped into. I thought that if a man

touched her
body there'd be a wreath
on the door, lemoncakes
on the table. I don't know
my belly from the wrought iron
heater, my hunger from the world's. I'm a suitcase

for a mind and mouth. As I try to hold
you, you must feel yourself falling
through me. What is the food

to fill me solid
as that woman's light?
I want to be a logger
in a gown. I want
to be the channel swimmer
toweled off, quiet, here with you.
I want to know I am—but I'm off

shopping at Bonwit's, stopping
at Dunkin Donuts. I eat three boxes
of animal crackers and study
the empty containers. I think I am

in a little corner of myself
in slippers in a great, an alarming
night. A shell—an ear, a mouth, telling
as a fashion magazine, deep
as a skillet. Oh, I'm deep

in trouble with my god. Scared
out of my mind
of you, I touch
your lucky flesh and for a second
there's the flash—incendiary:
trust, for a second
we're light, as we were meant to be
light, as we were born
in suits of light.
There's burning from beneath
brown skins,
a cup of water in my heart, joggling.

A MAJOR AMBITION

In my life: trying to avoid the marshmallow features, self
help books, hours spent
analogizing the soul, that it's like
drawings we did in kindergarten
where we'd color rainbows,
ink them over and scratch
designs through the ink, et cetera, that life
is ink and souls
are rainbows, ad, so on, infinitum. This
tedium of care bears
gone berserk, this is the fluff
of which my days seem made and I don't
like it, preferring
the genuines:
how to get the cat-piss smell
out of your carpet; how sunburns heal
acne; how feelings of shame
creep up, overwhelm, make us forget

God and our promises to Him, and remember,
physically re-experience, our fathers'
lectures in the den, what
lout heads, amount-to-nothings
we were, possibly
still are. Look:
I've only got one
of these lives and I want to try
to make it count, make it
actual, spend time lounging
with the white, the painfully
white budlings of snow, armloads
of lilac, the dreamy white inside
a strawberry, white puffs
of laughter drifting
over our grim jokes, laugh
of steeple bells
when they are far away,
shivering. And specific.

THAT IN HER

She watches from the upstairs room
two kids throw a book
from a car window, watches the wind
rifle and read. She thinks
she'd like to spend time gathering the lost
shoes and hats by the side of the road. So many
bottles, papers, the ginger movements and spindle
legs of the grazing deer, wild eyes of the struck
rabbits, the children joking, children
who survive, breath
on skin. . . . How can she possibly
contain this?
                     She looks
at the road, brings her nose
to the glass. Her face, torso, arms—she is
who the world sees, but I
am in her, watching
her watch: this road, its mitigated
horrors, the roads elsewhere, Belfast, Tel Aviv,
people marching. . . .
                     She tries to pull
herself shut, keep things
from touching, but still I am there. I don't know
what part, if I am bitter, frightened,
kind. . . . I am that
in her which opens
the window, letting the rain
rain in on her face
that has no skin. Urgent. And wanting
to be saved. Am I her heart? Or maybe
the one who wrings her heart.

CREATURE

It's raining but the cat
has to be convinced it's really
raining outside each door
on all four sides of the house and must be convinced
several times an hour. I get no work done,
but instead consider the operational logic
of this cat: "I want
to go out." No
polemics, no postulations. His needs
are simple and discussion
of cloud pattern, barometrics, providential
wheelings and dealings
isn't necessary. For me, the smart
one with bending thumbs, days

are more complex. The brain's taut
with language, can't be turned off, works
referentially, by memory, and not all memories
are pleasant. My brain feels scored
with petty infractions, pinholes
of various desertions, the one man
I loved. . . . I suffer from thought, my head
always a step behind
my life—I've already plunged
both hands into the steaming basin when I remember

pain. I'm a plodder and a planner,
but today I realize life's
gone on without me, head remote
from my heart, that lion
of the body. Dear heart, I like you:

pumping out, filling up, simple—alight
with water that can be seen through, rain
water, drops
the shape of candle flame.
Heart that is beast
like the cat: sees bird,
eats bird. No dissembling there, no
thinking it through. The heart falls
in love, rises
in love as the rain
falls, feeds, and invisibly
rises again. . . . Still,
I am that creature torn, a great
divide—even as I loved that man,
I stood apart, took notes
inside.

Obedience

The exquisite nail
of my denial has me. I am a thing
caught, with everyone else, trying to shove
off from love like a man
pushing away from a dock, swimming
beyond crying.

But pinned here
mercilessly, forced
across this parking lot
every morning, coffee and briefcase and wheeling
gulls overhead—so far
from the sea I can cry for them
in a way I can't
for you.

• • •

You whom I turn from.
You beside me
in countless Friday night
movie houses. You leaning
over the bureau.
You shaking out the newspapers.
Folded with sleep. The cat
you. The boy you.
You in the library. You appearing
in my office this morning, sitting
on my typing table. Sitting
and not saying. You who know.
You with me
through this bad time
of my bad throat, of my bad
bad heart that will not
break down and cry.
You whom I turn from
turning from my life.

• • •

In some way, we are all
obedient. Like it or not, we do
what God says. In this
we are nothing
more than shales on a roof, dainty scarves
tossed roadside. A brute necessity
kings us. But a worse
necessity: craving
what we fear, love—the stake soldered
to our spines and our one
straight up shot at freedom
not really free
since we are impelled. . . .

I make up that the gulls
are lost. They scream
as they fly. They
are broken-hearted. They swoop down
on dumped bags, cigarette
tinfoil, a broken-off door guard.
When I say I don't know
about love I mean
I don't even know
how to touch
my tongue to my lips
before beginning
to speak.

• • •

In a far more central
sea, in the matted down
brain, scientists say
is tissue in which emotions swim, and swam first—
swam before idea and word
and interpretation. First we felt
and then we thought
about what we felt—and then

we lifted off, grand, white
winged, best birds of earth we turned
from home. In this parking lot
I am alone. Only an act of God
can cure me, and so I ask
to be brought down, made
to feel my love for you, little firebrand,
little enemy, little bird.

ADRIFT

I was a lake this summer,
no oarsman. I was a lake totally
adrift with stars which seemed
pretty, their love excellent
and far. . . . Stars with veils, the wake
of oars upon their faces.
This summer I crossed
into love. Now

as autumn comes
I need to be lifted, carried
to the window. Forgive me
for depending on him.
Forgive me as I lean
and drift with fear.

I say that it's not love's
darkness but this
darkness that scares me: wanting
anyone at all. I'll try not to
make excuses. I'll just simmer
the beets and be quiet. I have admitted
need and need admits light
beneath the door: the door rows off
not saying much, a large white star casting
away from the imposition
need is, the burden
even words become
as love is taken on, as stars are
gathered in the boat
of one more thing
to say.

It was not the stars' silence.
It is not the silence now.
It's only that love went
to love's door and stood there
knocking. Ashamed, it admits
need, the shadow darker
than its own oar.

MICHAEL

Today the trees are blown, dumping their burnt leaves
unsensually as if it did not matter
how hard it is, how cell by cell, whit
by whit they are built.

Autumn. Trees are
weather here. I wonder if we
were ever sensual, one
to another. I wonder if we ever let
that thought cross our minds. Out the window,
the burial business. The relief.
As if we could dust off our hands
and be gone. As if we could

you have. Your ridiculous mug, your blue
typewriter, ashtray
smoldering, your arms, your hands, all
gone to 18 Stiles Street in a city
in a state
I know nothing about.

Here, we lie about seasons.
In fall we say: just look
how pretty, as if it is a bravery
to lie
about the fastidious reds
when we know
what's coming, how we blow and drift
and die of snow.

Nothing.
Nothing. We flash
our vacancies. It looks
like courage, this
lack of ambush, this refusal
to step into our lives, to say: Here, and with you. . . .

But go ahead. Move
somewhere else if you want to. Fill
your mug with coffee, hold
it, lean over
it. I'm staying

put. Leaves
cross and cross the road.
I want this difficulty
of staying, of loving and not
moving on. Leaves cross, make a shatter
of the landscape. I am made
and torn and made again. I am here
in my life
finally—where you can find me.

TWO

Now I am seeking the reason my life was in the world. . . .

—William Stafford

BOOK WITH FLOWER

At the window is just the thickness
of pines. I cannot charm myself
into believing anything more beneficent
about them but what is fact. Even now
the sap is slowing and the sun weakens
the hue of tree shadows so that one can only choose
between the semi-dark
and the semi-dark. That is
the kind of choice I made

in becoming your bride. There was a full blossoming
that was betrayal, a cutting away
of my life. Most of the time
I don't seem to know
how I got here—though, of course, I do;

at least, I've heard reports
that the flowers we left in the church
were used for a funeral three days later—which is typical
of God: always at the business
of turning that which is to endure
into that which has already
perished. It is only lately

I found the drawer with the book
into which a white rose has been pressed
these eight months. And still
I will happen awake in the midst
of some predictable task; I will turn off
the vacuum and sit down beside it, having suddenly
no understanding of its nature,
or my own, no sense
of how A leads to D. For a moment
it's like not living, this waking,
or, as if in order
to live, the events
of which we are composites must be given permission
to have occurred. . . .

Didn't we meet?
Didn't we say
we loved one another? Didn't we
get all dressed up one day? We did,
we married, didn't we?

Watching the gray edge of light—stock still
on the pine's still trunk—I think
that seasons are like money: how we wait and wait
for spring and when it arrives it's a loan
that has finally come through, the entire summer's
money in our pockets. . . . But autumn, this
November afternoon, I see

foreclosure upon foreclosure, everything
going pale and the children
beginning to starve again. Frequently
I go to the drawer

with the book with the flower inside. On this earth
if love does not repeat its name
it forgets
it is love. That's why

I open the drawer and why
I don't open the book. Secrets
are requisite to love; one does not want the bride
becoming wife too soon. . . . But that

must be how it ends. By next fall
I will have forgotten the drawer
and then, some day
that may be far away but exists
nevertheless
a flower

will fall from a book and we'll turn
to look for its stain
on one of the pages, not so much
to replace the flower as to wonder
how we ever arrived
at that page.

First House on Seth Street

It both is and is not
enough. Staying awake
while he sleeps, sleeping through
his wakefulness. . . . Of course,
love is not enough. There are swollen
shins from missed baseballs, eyes
unable to close upon themselves. There's
peanut butter in the cutlery drawer, incessant
worry that is nobody's
fault but hurts in my palms, in his
silent vernaculars. . . . We are
"even steven," both
lost to this grand world
of adjustment, both equipped
to do so much more
than adjust. . . . There is kindness. There is
the black-blue cloud of night.
We see lots of movies.
I call him by his name
but he is a boat
for me, a laundry line of flannels
singing the wind, waving empty
arms over the fence. He calls me: Bait, Scout,
Possum. We step carefully. We never name

the true name, we never say
that our hearts would bleed through our shirts
given a word—"leaving."
We're not
leaving. We're staying—but those words
break in us anyway as if that ending
had already occurred.

Reasons

The doctor's report arrived today
like the doctor himself, blowing
through the door—late, charming,
endlessly vague: "No
fetal autopsy was possible. . . ."
What does this mean, "possible"?
You call
from where it's freezing
rain changing to snow, say
you might be back Tuesday,
Wednesday. I see your face
asleep, arms asleep
on your face; your life,
I see it going on
without me. Why
this drift, this isolation? Because logic
can't persuade the heart
not to lower its wounded black
head, its white horns.
Because certain things happen
by chance and still
chance is not diminished:
we wanted this baby
and did not get him.
And I love you
and you love me.
And we did not get him.

THE INVISIBLE

As if the house has been broken into:
soft footfalls on the tile, a few grains
of sugar cascading down that safe
white mountain inside the checkered jar.
Would the geranium even tremble—disturbed
with air—if someone slipped
past, went up the gray steps, not to take
anything, but only to touch
the blue quilt cat on the bed, or stir
the dotted curtains just so—and so
to take what mattered?

Upstairs, he is still
in his crib, sleeping
before understanding
what has shaken from the house and yard all sense
of certainty, rustled
the swingset, distracting the dog from his watch
forever, altered
what this dreaming child
will come to dream. . . . His parents can't admit

this terror, the imagined
stealth, cruel,
ubiquitous—and exactly
in their denial does the seed
send out its white roots, giving a shape
to the invisible, effects
to what has, as yet, no cause. . . . They are so quiet
one almost wishes

to shake the plant
in its pretty pot, make it
open and speak
for the child's sake, splinter
the legs and arms of chairs,
hacking with a mallet until someone
cries out: that
can be fixed!
Can be replaced, and nothing
will be different, nothing. Or again
ever the same.

BRIGHT EYES

Finally, these days. The warm
we've waited for. How long ago
did we quietly tuck the baby
under the leaves and wreath
of fall flowers? The recluse cat
harbors himself under a deck chair.
You are gone for two weeks of chaplain's duty, sleeping
bag, pillow, camp
gear. I'm here, eyeing the cat
eyeing me. I feel this charade's
coming on, sitting in boxers
in a plastic swimming pool, the stubborn joke
of being determined to lose and not to grow
from loss. . . . Lettuce bends, bugs
abound, I really don't see
good reason. Call, give some.
Purple Impatiens, Bright Eyes, new grass
spikey under the sprinkler. Some clever rationale
escapes. Cistern summer, burial summer. Purples
and whites growing, you gone, no
way to reach, no word. The central eye
of the flower is pink, wet—
the whole of it hovers, still
expecting a simpler joy.

NIGHTS OF AUGUST

Around here, it comes and it goes. Goes
mostly. My nails are nubs, worrying
about the cat too near the road, deer ticks
invading every warm body that crosses
the lawn. My fault, I say, this house, this pulling
apart home. My own fault letting
the distance arrive so gradually and then
this suddenly.

I stand out on the porch nights
of August, with my husband, just to be near him.
Moths bat at my eyes. I go in, finish the dishes, he
finishes his book, all
business. All my body
asks is: are we all right?

I can hear him say it, deadpan: are we
all right. In a secret place, in the ruffian
clutch of my heart's bone I keep
hearing nope, nope. . . . I hear it
as I imagine Columbus heard:
there's *more*
to this earth. . . .

But if you were born on a planet they said
was flat, if you were born
to a world they said
was the center around which all the stars circled,
it would be hard to leave
that idea. Hard to go
from the pleasantries

into the tough cake. I don't want to look
at the waste. I hate being alone. Even now
I watch moths
spin about his cherub hands, his hair—even
now, I postpone. I once taped a note to my desk:
"What is right,
what is wrong, need we ask anyone to tell us
these things?"
I wait and watch because
I wish I had not
seen. Because the wind
feels huge, trackless. . . .
Because his one hand is milk, the other
snow—snow and milk on a planet
I have seen
is round and pulled
by the sun.

FORTUNE

Our green-white house
drifts downhill. All day,
all night, the lake water stirs below
with geese legs. Then suddenly the sky fills
with wing—Doug and I are earth-caught, somehow
diminished. Stories say
geese are luck; they bring
good fortune. We're sick
of pointing up, admiring. Sometimes
I swear we're secretly sick
of God, another beautiful
honker—who'll tear
saltines from your hand,
your heart from your collar. We think
about land-fills
and the lake, about saltines
and how hungry *we* are,
coming in from work: air
all wings, air
a dark old honking.
The sky is land
for rubber legs, cries
that pass over
our painted house and the chinese-red
swing on our porch, over
the rooftop where the bronze bird strains,
bound there to spin
in these changeable winds, a dervish
on an iron leg.

SEEDS

I plant them. I stick
my hands down there. I consider it
muck—worms and half
worms crawling away from my hefty
spoon. I dump sixty-eight more seeds
into this aggravating
earth. In December, my husband and I were having
a child. Now, it's summer and I keep sticking
stuff down and away. I make us
dinner: squash and beets, squash and beans. I apologize;
I attack. Nights, I look over at the clock
like I can't believe
it's not day. I say *shh* loudly so as not to be awake
alone. I think: big
deal. What you lost
wasn't even a kid, wasn't even good
like a flower. Wasn't
blue and low, deep
like your violas, your Johnny
Jump Ups, wasn't crisp, sandy, soily, green—green
and white as the asparagus, potato, uncle
basil. . . . My kitchen reels with the boiling

vegetables. My husband sleeps
sound through it. "Guilt's
too natural," he says, "a cliché. . . ."
We wanted something
we didn't get. Later,
there's talk and sense and trying
again. Right now, I just want
the flowers, to love
this garden I fill
and empty.

DECIDING ABOUT SILENCE

All day I have said and said.
It's January, medieval
cold out there and I'm sick of my voice:
"There, there. . . ." "Be nice." What
am I saying? I like the TV on
while my husband sleeps. It cries,
it weeps, he struggles
with the cat and hears
nothing. I'd like to say how badly
I feel, say how tired and a headache
all night, the vacuum cleaner sitting
in the dining room since Sunday, other
things. All day I have said.
Said to my students. To my son. To the dour
lady in the store. To my sleeping husband, I wanted to say
a kind, more feeling
thing—is it correct always
to speak? Is it right
to say what's going wrong? I stare
into my husband's ear and think about paper napkins,
picnics we've had together. Summers
come again. I guess what I'm saying is how
I feel like I failed. "Today," my husband would say

if he were awake, "just today. And it's not failing,
succeeding—we don't know
what those things are. It's the amount
of faith you had
when you spoke." I think about his ear,
about what I could stick
inside, a joke, a straw, the end
of a candle—and I decide about silence, decide
about that darkness where everything I love
sleeps; everything
I ever wanted
I have, except the sense
to hold still.

LOVE AND A WISH

My son is splayed
under tree branches, playing
with the light he believes he can hold
between infant fingers; husband nearby
planting pachysandra on the rocky hill
grass seasonally refuses—
nothing seems ever
to have been this
clear, this stunning
twin arrival of beauty and the desire
to be the lucky
predeceased.

HE SEES THINGS SMALL

I don't know what
he saw at first; theoretically
white and black, blurs
of face, coverlet, breast. Now
he sees things

small: the final raisin
on its plate, third luminant string
of his father's guitar that he longs
to pluck, a cat's whisker—

which is all I want him to see—
none of the victims, none
of the stacked bodies, not the second hand
sweeping us away. . . .

Teach him for me
not to trust love when it comes
like a desperate mother—its true face
and its blindfolds.

BLOOMS

When I tell you the news
you are glad, sweet, but still
out the door with briefcase and hat, leaving me
to do the same days over. Groceries,
diapers, laundry, lift, wipe, wipe, dragging
Peter who is rosy
with effort, his toddling unsteadied
by the wake of mommy's
active boredom. Parenthood must be this
state of being bereft, though the child remains
every wish granted. And now

a second one
is coming, another season
lost. I see the year ahead
as a great red bloom, some part of myself shaken
from its branch and put in a water jar—
this impossible apex of petals
opening, dropping. . . . It is good news
that saddens, the nature of beauty
to deprive.

No

I will not eat
those beans; they have hairs
on them. And no, I won't wear that pink
dress, pointy black shoes. Not
going to school. Won't wash my face.
I am hammering
gigantic dents into their headboards, pouring
lysol down my chin and telling them
I drank poison. Not unlocking
the bathroom door till I get my way. No,
I never understood how my father
kept his hair, why my mother's
didn't blanch.

Thirty years later, I am myself
"the meanest mommy." No, you can't
have your friends for the night. No TV.
No more popsicles. The little boy
takes himself upstairs to bed and I can imagine
his dreams: spider-infiltrated
attempts, escapes
to the land where he's king—outside
his room, I listen, the let me,
let me of his sleep. . . . What is *no*?

The blacksnake
of love, that lashing
sound in the air
which quickens us—he is getting ready
to lock the door, to stand
his ground and *no*
is my affirmation of this.
It is my blessing and my kiss,
my rough kiss.

PINK THING AT MID-LIFE

We joked about it
when we got engaged, how
I would become this
pink thing with fuzzy slippers
and curlers, toting the vacuum, dusting
the laundry hamper. . . .
But have you had a dream
you couldn't wake from, seen yourself slip
into an alien life? Or does it happen
by such increments
you can't see, don't remember
your dreams at all?

After the marriage, I wrote
letters, kept making the same typo:
"I have been marred
since June. . . ." Half of me
always tells the truth; half goes on,
becomes a teacher, writes
more letters, has children and takes them
to Schultz's Apple Farm. The years
feel soft and hazy, imprecise
but busy with concerns
about safety wheels, gas heat—I have concerns
about this lack of feeling, lack

of singular concern. Can a life
disappoint itself? Is there someone else
I meant to be? Half of me
can't live the way I live, in this abandonment
of jelly jars and cleaning fluids.
I am looking at myself and judging.
I am the judge of pink things,
in halves, awakened
by the middle of my life.

• • •

You say: it's not so bad.
You say: look around.
But I can't bear
this mitigation, the holes
in our lives plugged up
with little corks. I don't want
to be president, don't
want to be on TV. I'd just like
one day of life to be real, with us really
in it, talking, driving, actually
smoking the cigarettes we smoke.
I want a heart for a heart instead of a brain.

I want a bird to land on a tree
that's never been landed on. I want that connection
to life. I want that connection to life
to be clear.
Not so much to change
as to acknowledge. Own up.
To say yes, I am a housewife:
I have curlers and a hairnet. Yes,
I am average, not young,
not old, not fat or thin,
not beautiful and yet,
not impressive and yet. . . . By all appearances

I have settled for less
and I am saying it's not a question
of less. It's seeing
who I am, framing that,
like a work of art,
with this body and walking
into the world—not at peace,
but home, at last.

FUR

She wears elegant black, perfume
over her perfume and furthermore
is beautiful. I'm polite, even
entertaining. Between her perfect ankles
I spot the cat under the couch, eyes yellow, radar
ears swiveling, the picture
of wild fear calmly
licking its favorite mink, its superior
stole. When she leaves,
I tell the cat, we'll go out,
shred a few starlings.

Perfect Life

Some nights he'll ask me. He'll notice
how wisk by wisk my hair
has come askew, how my shirt buttons
are gray with lunch sauce and he'll say: apoplexy
doesn't become you, honey,
before he turns, sleeps.

And suddenly I'm the child again.
Any response I could possibly, lengthily,
logically assemble
puts me in the back seat of the car
with the suitcases and panting dog, my parents threatening
to leave me on the highway if I don't stop doing
whatever it was I was
doing that made me such a trial,
a less than perfect
little girl. I cry
in a stupid way. I cry poorly, I weep
because I want to.

I pull off shoes, on socks,
tinker with my hair. I horrify
myself: dabs of toothpaste, cut off
nightgown. I look in
the mirror and think: this face
will take years to fix. . . . My heart,
a smaller, deeper weight, gives up, kisses
off or whatever kids are saying today
that means diminished.

I stare at his huge lashes. They reach his nose
almost. I think about the peeling shingles
of this house, the money, glue, taxes.
"If you touch me," I whisper,
"you're a dead man." After work,
after two meetings, after the car oil light
flashed on and off and on, can't I just be asleep

like him? I'm tired
of not understanding
why we both come home each night.
I nudge him
a little, I wake him, say, "Were you
awake?" Just so

he'll turn over again, grab me, kiss
and kiss me. He makes love
to me. I can't
understand: how he loves me. . . . It must be
a mistake. It doesn't seem correct,
there are inconsistencies here.
Here in this life of ours.
In this perfect life.

STUPID CHICKEN FALLS IN LOVE

Standing in the wrong
line at the check-out, cashier
screaming to the manager: "Void!
I've got a void here. . . ," I have plenty
of time to scan headlines
in the racks. NATIONAL
ENQUIRER, STAR, WEEKLY WORLD full
of Elvis sightings, miracle
cancer cures, Carmelite
nun forced to make love to space
visitors, and this: Stupid
Chicken Falls In Love
With Pick-Up Truck.

I think I ought to be
above all this, our gumball
world, its schlock
and tack. I want disdain
enough to turn away—

but frankly all my life
I've turned away
from seeing what I am: expert
in the art of hedging, acting
like an "educated" person with a little

dough, some sort
of fucking privilege that shelters me,
makes me better, far
too cool to care
about nuns and loud cashiers, beyond belief
in Elvis or these shopping carts of whining
kids and melted fudgsicles. . . . Inside,

I'm runny as an egg, ashamed; afraid
you'll find me out, I hide
in self-help books that say:
I should assert, suspect, avoid
dependencies of any sort, look out
for numero uno, take care
of my needs, my
cholesterol, my lingerie—seriously,
who hasn't, just once, pretended
to be clean of earth, inviolable, a perfect
fartless specimen?

It doesn't matter what
wakes us, or when, so long as we do
wake and step
into our lives—here, in this supermarket
I stir, arouse and see: one

Nebraska prairie chicken. White feathers
all fluffed out, air sac
on his neck inflated, he hoops and stamps—
a loaded diaper on two pocked legs—
this prairie courtship dance
every time the blue Dodge truck
comes home across the meadow. All night
the bird roosts inside that paneled cab, soft smell
of cows and plastic, far light
of stars. . . . While in the house the farmer lies
beside his cranky
comfortable wife, smiling, strangely attached

to this chicken who stoops so low
to love. What does this farmer in Nenzel
know? I stare
at the cashier, her tinted hair, mouth
snapping gum, eyes caked
with Maybelline. I stare at her to whom

I'm kin. Our skin and veins and genitals
connecting us, relatives
to bat and buffalo, iguana, antelope, house
cat, the man
who runs the heavy print machine, the secretary

with the twitch, and I say here's
to it—what
connects us in our differences; here's to
our blood and tenderness, to sobbing
at the matinee, to tears and noses
wiped across our sleeves.
To dependent relationships—the pain they cause!
To the human mind ever-inventing
nuclear fission and the lobster bib—
to Beckett's sadness and the snow
on Issa's cheek, to our common
elements and to
the chicken, the stupid, enthusiastic
chicken who fell beyond himself and loved
a pick-up truck—to the farmer,

asleep by now, who knows
just what he knows: that food
comes up out of the earth
and we go down into it,
that we are brief, and love,
whatever of, is love.

Kate Knapp Johnson attended Middlebury College, Columbia University's School of the Arts, and received her MFA from Sarah Lawrence College. Her first book, *When Orchids Were Flowers*, was published in 1986 (Dragon Gate, Inc.). A recipient of a 1989 New York Foundation of the Arts Award, she currently teaches creative writing at Sarah Lawrence College and lives in Mt. Kisco, NY with her husband and son.